Battersea Dogs & Cats Home

Caring for CATS and KITTENS

Ben Hubbard

W
FRANKLIN WATTS
LONDON•SYDNEY

Contents

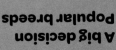
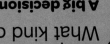
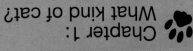
This edition published in 2015
by Franklin Watts

Franklin Watts
338 Euston Road
London NW1 3BH

Franklin Watts Australia
Level 17/207 Kent Street
Sydney, NSW 2000

Text copyright © Franklin Watts 2014

Produced under licence from Battersea Dogs
Home Ltd. ® Battersea Dogs & Cats Home

Royalties from the sale of this book go
towards supporting the work of Battersea
Dogs & Cats Home (Registered charity no
206394) **battersea.org.uk**

Series editor: Sarah Peutrill
Series designer: Matt Lilly
Cover designer: Cathryn Gilbert
Picture researcher: Diana Morris
Photographs: Clint Singh,
unless otherwise stated
Illustrations: Jason Chapman

The Author and Publisher would like to thank
the staff of Battersea Dogs & Cats Home for
their guidance with this book.

Picture credits:
Illustrations © Jason Chapman 2014
Photographs © Clint Images/Battersea Dogs
& Cats Home 2014, unless otherwise stated
(see page 64)

Every attempt has been made to clear
copyright. Should there be any inadvertent
omission please apply to the publisher
for rectification.

Dewey number: 636.8'083
ISBN: 978 1 4451 2780 4
Printed in China

Franklin Watts is a division of Hachette
Children's Books,
an Hachette UK company.
www.hachette.co.uk

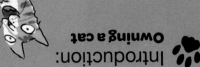

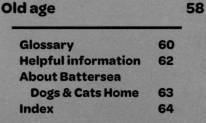

Introduction : Owning a cat

Cats have lived with people for thousands of years. Long ago, farmers liked cats because they killed rats and other rodents. Soon, cats were curled up in human homes. Some ancient cultures even worshipped cats! Today, cats are our furry friends, our cuddly companions and our perfect pets. Are you ready to take care of a cat?

Owning a cat is a big commitment. It means looking after the cat's health, safety and happiness for the whole of her life. Before getting a cat, ask yourself the following questions. If the answer to any of them is "no", then you're probably not ready for a cat. If your answer is always "yes", then read on to learn how to care for your cat in the best possible way.

Will I care for her?

Cats need to be fed, groomed and taken to the vet when they are sick. They also need someone to play with them!

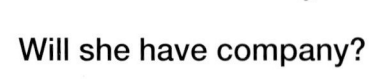

Will she have company?

Kittens need constant care for the first few months. Adult cats need people around too. It's not fair to leave a cat by herself all day, every day. There must be someone at home at least in the morning and evening to keep her company.

Will I clean up after her?

Kittens have to be housetrained. All cats need their litter trays cleaned out. They also need someone to vacuum up their stray hairs!

Will I be patient?

Cats are independent creatures and don't always do what you want. You have to let them do things in their own time, at their own pace. They may also claw your family's furniture and curtains!

Will the answer to these things be "yes" for 14 years or more?

This is the average length of a cat's life. Some cats can even live to over 20! Owning a cat is an enjoyable adventure. But you have to be prepared to go the distance.

Top tip!

Get your whole family involved in answering these questions. You'll need their help with your cat too. Also, before getting a cat make sure no-one has a cat allergy by making sure the whole family has spent time with cats.

Chapter 1: What kind of cat?

🐾 A big decision

Choosing a pet cat is a big decision. Would you like a pedigree cat or a moggy? A male or a female? Is an adult cat better than a kitten? Can you have an indoor or an outdoor cat? As you read about these different types of cat, think about which would best suit your family life and home.

A moggy or pedigree?

Moggies are cats which come from an unknown mixture of breeds. For this reason, moggies all have different coat colours, fur lengths and character traits. Pedigree cats come from parents of the same breed. They share their breed's looks and character traits. Pedigrees sometimes need extra grooming and can suffer more from health problems. Moggies are usually easy to care for and less prone to illness.

Male or female?

There are few differences between male and female cats that have been neutered. Neutering is a common operation to stop cats producing kittens (see pages 50–51). Unneutered males spend time looking for female cats and often spray indoors to mark their territory. They also fight with unneutered male cats. Unneutered female cats can be noisy and have to be kept inside while 'in season'.

A kitten or an adult?

Kittens are cute and cuddly, but they can be a lot of work! They have to be housetrained, fed more often than adults, and can claw furniture. Somebody also has to stay at home to care for a kitten during the first few months. Less work is needed with adult cats, who have usually been neutered, housetrained and are used to living with people. But adults have grown up personalities so it can take longer to teach them new things.

An indoor or outdoor cat?

Indoor cats usually spend their lives inside because their owners live in a building with no outside space. Cats infected with the disease FeLV also need to be kept indoors (see pages 48–49). Indoor cats can enjoy a good quality of life, but depend on their owners for their exercise and entertainment. Indoor cats need lots of fun and games, or they become bored, frustrated and overweight.

🐾 Popular breeds

When choosing a pedigree cat, it is helpful to know about the care each breed will need and its particular character traits. A character trait is a typical behaviour. The more you know about a cat, the easier it is to find the best match for you. The following table shows some of the United Kingdom's most popular cat breeds.

Breed		Description
	Abyssinian	Graceful and slender with long legs and almond-shaped eyes.
	Bengal	Long body and a striking coat with leopard-like markings.
	Birman	Large, strong and stocky with long, silky fur.
	British Shorthair	Short and strong, with a thick tail and round face.
	Burmese	Muscular, with a short coat and big expressive eyes.
	Exotic Shorthair	Average-sized, with big eyes and a medium-length coat.
	Maine Coon	Large and powerful, with tall, upright ears and a long coat.

Traits	Care needed
Intelligent, curious, sociable and cautious.	Human company and access to trees or other climbing places.
Intelligent, love water, vocal and always ready to play.	Active hunters so must have a large garden, with plenty of space to roam. Best suited to homes outside towns and cities.
Curious, affectionate and good with children.	Lots of attention, or the Birman will demand it!
Easy-going, loyal and happy around other pets and children.	Very little grooming but needs lots of company.
Lively, vocal, playful and adapts well to busy families.	Lots of play and affection or can become mischievous.
Fun-loving, loyal, quiet and peaceful.	Regular grooming to stop a matted coat.
A sweet natured, calm and friendly 'gentle giant'.	Loves hunting and stalking.

Breed	Description
Oriental	Slender, with a wedge-shaped face and tall upright ears.
Persian	Short and stocky body with a thick coat.
Ragdoll	Large and muscular with long fur and a bushy tail.
Russian Blue	Sleek, with striking emerald-green eyes and a smiling mouth.
Siamese	Long, slender body with vivid blue eyes.
Turkish Van	Strong and sturdy with a silky coat and furry paws.
Moggy (also known as a non-pedigree, Mongrel or domestic cat)	All different shapes, sizes, colours and fur lengths.

Traits	Care needed
Vocal, energetic and loves entertaining.	Lots of attention or will become fed-up and depressed.
Playful, laidback and easily adjusts to new places.	Lots of grooming to keep the coat clean and untangled.
Calm, affectionate and good around children and other pets.	Lots of grooming and extra games to keep her fit.
Affectionate, cautious and sometimes shy.	Loves routine but dislikes changes to its home environment.
Vocal, affectionate and hates being left alone.	Lots of company or will become loud and demanding.
Friendly, lively and loves playing in water.	Needs extra grooming to prevent a matted and tangled coat.
A mixture of character traits.	Lots of care, attention and love – like all cats.

Chapter 2: Choosing your cat

🐾 The best places

There are many different places to find a pet cat. The best places are rescue centres, pedigree breeders, or anyone that has cared for the cat, had her vet-checked (see page 48) and wants to find her a good home. Make sure you are happy with the place and people you are getting your cat or kitten from.

Do your research

It's important to know the cat you are picking is healthy and free from disease. Unfortunately, many people breed cats to make money and do not care about their health or welfare. Often their cats have been badly treated and are infected with diseases. It is therefore best to avoid buying a cat from newspaper advertisements, car-boot sales and pet shops, and to be careful when buying one from the Internet. Only buy cats from dedicated cat websites that encourage them to be fully health checked, neutered and microchipped (see page 62). Cats from respectable rescue centres will have been vaccinated, microchipped and well cared for. The same should be expected from a good pedigree breeder.

It's worth talking to a vet about good rescue centres and pedigree breeders in your area.

Rescue cats

Rescue centres, such as Battersea Dogs & Cats Home, rehome thousands of cats and kittens every year. By rehoming, you can offer a homeless or unwanted cat a brand new start. Rescue cats come in a range of different types, sizes, colours and ages. There are also cat breed rescue centres, that rehome pedigree cats and kittens. If you decide to rehome a rescue cat, staff at the centre will interview you to find the cat that is the best fit. You'll also get time to play with the cat to see if you like each other.

Ask the expert!

Q

What if a cat adopts me?

A

Sometimes cats will roam around their neighbourhoods looking for an extra meal. For this reason, you should never feed a visiting cat. Instead, try and find her owner and explain what is happening. If you think the cat is a genuine stray, you can talk to your vet or a local rescue centre about rehoming her.

🐾 Which cat to pick?

When picking out a pet cat, it's best to choose one with the right temperament for you. Temperament is an animal's nature and every cat has a different one. They can be energetic or lazy, loud or quiet, confident or shy. By spending time with a cat you'll soon see her true temperament shining through.

By playing with all of the kittens you'll find the best one for you.

Picking a kitten

If you are getting a kitten from an individual or a pedigree breeder, it is always best to visit them in their home. It's important that the kitten has been brought up in a home environment similar to yours. The kittens should be confident around people and familiar with normal day-to-day noises. The mother should be there with her kittens, and all should look healthy, well-cared for and happy. If you are picking your kitten from a rescue home, the staff may be able to tell you about your kitten's background. Make sure you always spend a good amount of time with a kitten, so you can watch her play and see what her temperament is like.

Kitten checklist

Before choosing a kitten, make sure she:

🐾 Is over nine weeks of age.

🐾 Has been raised in the same place that she was born.

🐾 Has been weaned and is eating solid food.

🐾 Has been vaccinated.

🐾 Has registration documents (if a pedigree kitten).

🐾 Moves about easily and freely.

Adult cat checklist

If you are getting an adult cat from a respectable rescue centre, she will have been microchipped, neutered and had her vaccinations. If you are getting an adult cat from another source, make sure she:

- 🐾 Breathes normally without wheezing or coughing.
- 🐾 Has a well-groomed coat without bald patches.
- 🐾 Has clear eyes without discharges.
- 🐾 Is clear of sores, damaged paws and inflamed gums.
- 🐾 Moves about easily and freely.

An adult cat should look healthy – don't pick an unhealthy one because you feel sorry for her.

Top tip!

It is important that a kitten is exposed to lots of different people, animals and things when she is young. This process is called socialisation. Well-socialised cats are less frightened by new things and are more friendly around people and pets.

Chapter 3: Bringing your cat home

🐾 Get prepared

It's important to get your home ready for your cat before she arrives. You will need a cat bed, food and bowls, a collar and ID tag, a litter tray and a cat carrier to transport her. You will also need to make your home safe for your new pet.

A cat bed

You can buy your cat a ready-made bed, or make one from a cardboard box. Cut one side off the box so your cat can get in and out. Then put newspapers underneath the bed to keep it off the floor. Finish the bed with a warm, washable blanket.

Cat identity

Your cat should wear a collar and identity tag, so you can be contacted if she gets lost. Buy a quick-release safety collar, so your cat can wriggle free if she gets caught. Make sure you can slip two fingers between the collar and your cat's neck. You can also microchip your cat. This involves inserting a microchip under the skin of your cat's neck. The microchip can be scanned to access your details from a database (see page 62 for microchipping).

Carriers

The best cat carriers are made from plastic and wire mesh with an easily removable lid on the top. This makes it easy to lift you cat in and out. Avoid cardboard carriers, which can be easily chewed and are impossible to clean if your cat goes to the toilet.

Litter trays

There are many types of litter tray available, including open and covered trays. Use non-scented litter of the same type your cat has been using in her old home. Cats like privacy when going to the toilet, so keep your litter tray somewhere quiet and out of the way (see pages 26–27 for housetraining).

A cat-proof home

Cats are great explorers and love to investigate anything new. Make your home safe by keeping toilet seats down, rubbish bins covered, washing machine and tumble dryer doors shut and windows closed. Also keep cleaning products, plastic bags, house plants and cut flowers out of reach. (Some cut flowers, especially lilies, are poisonous to cats.)

Top tip!

Buy non-slip food and water bowls and make sure your cat always has fresh water.

🐾 The first day

Bringing your cat home is the exciting moment you've been waiting for, but for your cat, travelling in a car to a strange, new place can be a bit scary. When she arrives, it is important to give your cat a quiet and gentle welcome to her new home.

One room

Keep your new cat in one room for the first few days. The room should be warm and quiet and have your cat's bed, litter tray, food and water bowls. For the first day, it is best if you are the only person who stays in the room with her. Make sure the doors and windows are shut, and that there are no tight spots where she can get stuck. When you let your cat out of her carrier don't approach, but talk gently so your cat becomes used to your voice. Keep an eye on your cat, but let her investigate things by herself. She will come and say hello once she has settled and feels safe. Make sure your cat has some food and water, and let her sleep if she wants to.

Your cat's reaction

Cats take time to adjust to a new place, so don't panic if yours seems shy or stressed. She may try and escape, or find a hiding place where she can safely check things out. She may also creep around with her body low to the ground, lick her lips, and even hiss or spit. These are all normal signs she is nervous, so let her know that you are friendly. Talk in a calm, comforting voice and don't stare at her – especially if she is watching from a hiding place. When she is ready to approach you, glance at her and then look away and blink slowly. She may do the same. This is how cats say "hello". You could then put a little tinned tuna on the floor near you, which she will find hard to resist!

Top tip!

If your cat already has a blanket, put this on her bed without washing it. The scents on the blanket will make her feel more at home.

🐾 Meeting the family

If your cat seems settled and relaxed after her first day, then she can be introduced to the rest of your family. Everyone will be excited and eager to meet your new pet. But make sure they all know some basic cat safety before being introduced.

Start quietly

Your family should meet your cat in the room where she is spending her first few days. Here, they should sit quietly and let the cat approach them. Lots of people calling out and moving around may scare your cat. Adults should always be present when your cat is around small children, especially if she is a kitten. It is important that small children do not tease your cat and learn how to hold her correctly. It is best not to introduce your cat to any existing pets in the house until she is used to your family.

Cat dos and don'ts

- 🐾 Always be quiet and gentle around your new cat.
- 🐾 Don't stare at your cat.
- 🐾 Let your cat approach you in her own time.
- 🐾 Don't disturb your cat if she is eating or sleeping.
- 🐾 Don't drag your cat out from a tight spot – tempt her out with a treat instead.
- 🐾 Stroke your cat's fur in the direction it grows and avoid her face and stomach.
- 🐾 Always let your cat move away from you if she wants to.

Holding your cat

Always pick your cat up gently and never grab her suddenly without warning.

1 Pat or stroke her gently.

2 Put one hand under your cat's chest and the other under her back legs.

3 Lift her carefully.

4 Hold your cat against your body, so she feels safe. Let her get down if she wants to.

Top tip!

If your cat rubs her head on you she is rubbing on her scent, as if to say: "You belong to me!"

Ask the expert!

Q

What should I do if my cat miaows during the night?

A

Always take her to the vet if this is new behaviour. But, as long as she doesn't have any medical issues, just let her calm down by herself. Leaving a warm hot-water bottle in her bed at night can help comfort her. If you think she is bored, leave some new toys for her.

🐾 Meeting other pets: dogs

Keep your existing pets away from your new cat for the first few days. You can make your pets aware of each other by rubbing rags on their coats and leaving them around the house. Keep the first introductions short and sweet, and make both animals feel equally loved.

Meeting your dog

You can make your cat feel safe around your dog by providing an escape route to somewhere she can hide. If she can get up somewhere high she will feel safer. You could also use a kitten pen so she feels protected (see opposite). Make sure your dog and new cat are as relaxed as possible before introducing them.

1 Ensure you have exchanged scents (as mentioned above) before the first actual meeting.

2 Take your dog into the room on a lead.

3 Let your cat approach the dog. Keep the dog next to you, on a short lead. If your cat is frightened or not interested, leave some treats for the cat, and repeat again the next day. Your cat may hiss or swipe your dog's nose, so have a firm grip on the lead at all times.

4 If your cat and dog are getting along, let the dog's lead go slack. Call him away from your cat from time to time and give him a treat, and give plenty of treats to your cat.

5 Repeat this introduction twice a day for a few days. If your cat and dog stay relaxed with each other, let them spend time together freely.

Kitten pens

A kitten pen is a large wire cage that your cat cannot escape from. It is a useful place to leave your kitten briefly if you can't watch over her. Make sure the pen is large enough to fit your cat's bed, her litter tray, and her food and water bowls. Kitten pens are helpful when meeting existing pets, as your new cat is completely protected inside. A pen should never be used for long periods of time, or to lock up a naughty kitten.

Ask the expert!

Q

What if my cat and dog don't get on?

A

Separate your cat and dog immediately if they become angry with each other and repeat the introduction the next day. Most cats and dogs learn to tolerate each other, even if they don't become best buddies!

🐾 Meeting your pets: cats

The first meeting between your new cat and your existing cat should be taken slowly and smoothly. Even if both cats have lived with other cats in the past, it doesn't mean they will get on. Make sure both animals have easy escape routes and don't try and force them to become friends.

Introducing your cats

Your existing cat will probably have spent time sniffing around the door of your new cat's room. Make sure this door is kept shut for the first couple of days while your new cat settles in. Then, with the help of two adults (one for each cat) get ready for the two cats to meet.

1 Open the door slightly so your existing cat can see your new cat.

2 Allow your existing cat to enter your new cat's room and let them check each other out. There may be some hissing and grumbling, but this is normal.

3 If your existing cat goes up to sniff your new cat, let her. If there is any aggression, drop a set of keys to distract them. If they really start to fight badly and nothing else works, you can also spray them with a water pistol.

It is up to your cats to decide if they like each other.

4 After a couple of minutes end the introduction by taking your existing cat out of the room. Give both cats a treat and lots of praise.

Repeat this introduction until the cats are used to each other. When this happens you can let your new cat explore the rest of the house, while you keep your existing cat in one room. Then, let both cats around each other freely. Make sure you feed your cats in different places to start with and separate them immediately if there is trouble.

Top tip!

If both your existing cat and your new cat use litter trays make sure they have one tray each. As with their food and water bowls, keep the litter trays in different parts of the house so they do not become protective over them.

Bringing your cat home **25**

Chapter 4: Housetraining

 Easy to train

Cats are clean creatures who are careful about where they go to the toilet. This makes them easy pets to housetrain. During the first few weeks, provide your cat with a litter tray while she is kept inside. By putting her litter tray in the right spot, your cat will soon learn to use it.

A quiet spot

While your cat is being kept in one room for the first few days, put her litter tray as far away from her bed and food bowl as possible. Once she is allowed around the rest of the house, put the litter tray somewhere quiet and private where she won't be disturbed. It should be away from her bed and food and water bowls.

Housetraining steps

Try and predict when your cat will need to go to the toilet so you can help housetrain her.

❶ After eating, sleeping and play, call your cat to the litter tray.

❷ Encourage her into the tray and praise her when she does.

❸ When she goes to the toilet, give her a treat.

Litter trays

The best litter trays are simple covered or uncovered models that are easy to clean. Use the same unscented litter your cat used in her old home, and make sure it is changed regularly. Cats will not use a tray they feel is dirty or smelly. Add soil and grass to her litter tray a few days before she is allowed outside. When she is let out, place the tray outside too. Most cats will naturally find a spot outside and forget about the litter tray.

Some cats prefer a more private, covered litter tray.

Ask the expert!

Q

What happens if my cat goes to the toilet outside of her litter tray?

A

Make sure you don't scold or punish her, or going to the toilet will make her nervous. If possible, move the litter tray to wherever she is going. The tray may be somewhere she doesn't like. If this is a new behaviour, or if it continues, it is best to ask your vet for advice.

Top tip!

Clean any cat mess with citrus-based cleaning products (cats don't like the smell) recommended by your vet. This will stop her going in the same spot again. Avoid strong chemicals like bleach.

Chapter 5: Food and feeding

🐾 A balanced diet

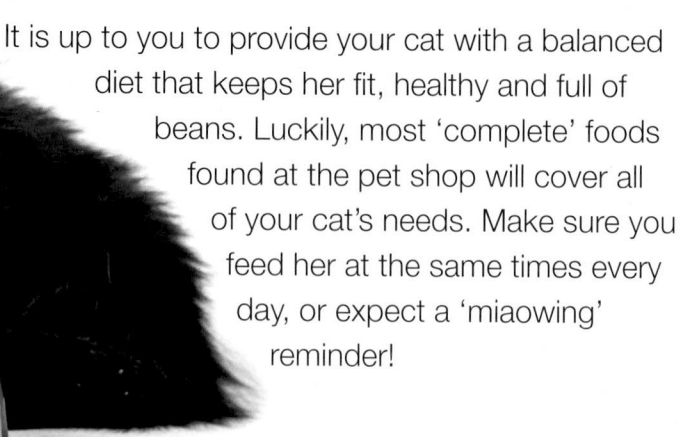

It is up to you to provide your cat with a balanced diet that keeps her fit, healthy and full of beans. Luckily, most 'complete' foods found at the pet shop will cover all of your cat's needs. Make sure you feed her at the same times every day, or expect a 'miaowing' reminder!

What to feed your cat

'Complete' dried and wet foods are equally healthy, so let your cat decide which she likes best. Dried food can be left in your cat's food bowl all day, so she can eat whenever she likes. If you have two or more cats, however, make sure they all get their share, and that one cat isn't taking all of it! Your cat will also not eat anything she doesn't like. If she walks away from her food try using a different type or flavour.

Wet food.

Dried food.

Dinner time

Feed your cat in a quiet place where she won't be disturbed. A metal or ceramic bowl with a rubber-rim doesn't move around easily. Remember to keep the bowl clean. Have a second bowl always filled with fresh water. When your cat's meal is ready, make a sound that acts as her dinner bell. You could tap on her tinned food with a spoon or shake her dried food box as you call her name.

How much food?

The amount of food your cat needs depends on her weight and her age. Adult cats should be fed twice daily, while kittens often need up to four small meals a day. To calculate how much food your cat needs, simply follow the guidelines on your chosen 'complete' food label. If you need to weigh your cat, do so by holding her as you stand on some bathroom scales. Simply take off your own weight from the total to find out how much your cat weighs. 'Complete' foods are also available for a cat's changing needs, such as when she ages, or is lacking in a particular food group. Make sure to talk to your vet about your cat's diet whenever you visit.

Your cat may appear to ask for more food, but in fact, she may just need a cuddle.

Top tip!

Some cats prefer to drink from a running water source such as from taps or water fountains. All cats need fresh water every day.

Chapter 6: Play and exercise

🐾 Fun and games

There are few things more fun than playing games with your cat. Play brings out the hunter in cats, and lets them stalk, chase and pounce like they are in the wild. Make sure you play with your cat every day and provide some toys for extra excitement.

Toys

Cats love toys, especially those they can bat, roll and jump on. Balls, fluffy mice and toys on strings are particular favourites. You can also make your own toys. A simple, scrunched-up newspaper ball tied to a piece of wool can provide hours of fun for you and your cat. A ping-pong ball bounced between family members is another cheap and easy game to play. Learn which toys your cat likes best and keep some of them hidden after

play, so they stay interesting. Make sure you never leave a string toy lying around, it can seriously hurt your cat if she swallows it.

Cardboard fort

Cats love cardboard boxes, and can spend hours entertaining themselves jumping in and out of them. Make a fort for your cat by cutting holes in a cardboard box for her to jump through (ask an adult to help). You could also paint the fort or make a special roof for it. Leave a treat inside the fort every now and then for her to discover.

Catnip toys

Catnip is a herb that makes cats playful. Cat treats are often made with catnip, and your cat will love fishing them out of a ball dispenser toy.

Scratching post

A scratching post is an important toy for your cat to sharpen her claws on. It also helps save your family's furniture. If you see your cat scratching the furniture tell her "no" and put her by the scratching post instead.

Top tip!

Never use your fingers for your cat to attack or chase, or this will become a bad habit.

🐾 Going outside

After around four weeks of being kept inside, you can introduce your cat to the outside world. For a kitten, you will have to wait until two weeks after she has been neutered and had her final vaccinations. Keep the first few outside visits short, so your cat can adjust slowly.

First visit outside

Your cat's first visit outside should take place 10 minutes before her dinner. Open the door into your garden so your cat can go out if she wants to. Your cat will be nervous, so let her know you are close by. After 10 minutes outside, make your cat's dinner bell sound (see pages 28–29) so she knows it's time to eat. Keep her inside for the rest of the day. The next day, let your cat have 20 minutes outside and keep extending her visits by 10 minutes a day. Once she seems relaxed outside, you can introduce her to a cat flap (see pages 34–35).

Indoor cats

If you do not have any outside space or your cat has FeLV (see page 48), she will need to stay indoors. When most cats are being let outside for the first time, you should help your indoor cat practise her natural outdoor behaviour. To do this, you can create a play area for your cat. You can buy special indoor 'cat trees' for your cat to climb up, or make something similar from a step ladder. Always ask an adult to help you with this. Play lots of chasing games with toys on strings, so your cat gets a chance to play at hunting.

Ask the expert!

Q

Will my kitten be safe outside?

A

Yes – the outside world is a cat's natural environment. But to start with, stay close by to help her get used to this big, new place.

Top tip!

Make sure your cat has been microchipped and has a collar and ID tag before going outside for the first time.

 Cat flaps

A cat flap is like your cat's key to the back door. It lets her go outside and come back in whenever she pleases. Once your cat understands the cat flap, she will use it without a second thought. But to start with, you will have to show her how it works.

Many cats learn that cat flaps are not the only way to get out!

Which type?

There are many types of cat flap available, all of which fit into an outside door. The most basic models are plastic flaps that move backwards and forwards, so your cat can go out and come back in. Other cat flaps have a setting that allows your cat only to go one way through the flap. At the top of the range are unique key-coded cat flaps, that are connected to an infra-red device on your cat's collar. When your cat approaches such a cat flap, it opens automatically. This means no strange cats can enter the house through the cat flap.

Cat flap training

To start with, cats are often nervous of the way a cat flap swings backwards and forwards. Show your cat the cat flap will not harm her using the following steps.

1 Tape the cat flap open, or prop it open with a stick.

2 Sit on the opposite side of the open cat flap to your cat, and use a treat to coax her through.

3 Go around to the other side of the open cat flap, and coax her through again.

4 Untape the flap or remove the stick. Push the flap to show your cat that it opens.

5 Go around to the other side of the open cat flap, and coax her through with a treat as before. Encourage and praise your cat as she pushes the flap open. Keep changing sides until she has got the hang of going through it.

Ask the expert!

Q Should I lock my cat out at night?

A No, this is not fair on your cat and unnecessary if you have a cat flap in place.

The scared cat

A scared cat will crouch down and tuck herself in. Her ears will be flat and her eyes wide open and looking away. A scared cat is usually ready to back away, so it is best not to approach one. Do not even look in a scared cat's direction, or this may scare her more. Scared cats can also become aggressive, so if you want to stroke or comfort one try calling her instead of approaching.

The relaxed cat

A relaxed cat walks easily on all fours with an upright tail that does not twitch or swish. Her ears will be upright, alert and pointed forward. She will narrow her eyes and hold eye contact to show that she trusts you and feels safe. Most relaxed cats are happy for people to approach them to be stroked or play a game.

Cats 'speak' using vocal sounds, facial expressions and body language. Often, when your cat moves her eyes, ears, mouth, tail and paws, she is talking to you. As you get to know your cat, you will understand what this body language means. Before then, there are three simple body language poses that are easy to recognise.

🐾 Body language

Chapter 7: Understanding your cat

The angry cat

An angry cat will arch her back, swish her tail and extend her claws. The fur on her back and neck will stand on end, and she will open her mouth to bare her teeth. An angry cat's ears will be turned back, which shows she is ready for an attack. It is important never to approach an angry cat. Don't shout, scream or run, but instead walk away quietly.

Ask the expert!

Q Do all cats use the same vocal sounds to say the same thing?

A

No. From low grumbling to high pitched whines, cats have a range of vocal sounds that each one uses differently. Watch what your cat is doing when she makes her vocal sounds to figure out what she is saying to you.

Top tip!

If you are ever unsure about what a cat is trying to say to you, ignore her and walk away. If she wants your attention she will follow you.

🐾 Why does my cat ... ?

Cats can be confusing creatures. They purr, rub against things, and knead their paws into our laps. They seem to sleep all the time, but then wake up at night to play and hunt. Why do they do these things? Here are answers to some of the most common questions about our feline friends.

Why does my cat purr?

Cats usually purr when they are happy, relaxed or being stroked by their owner. Sometimes an ill or anxious cat purrs as well. Cats start purring when they are kittens, to let their mother know that they are suckling her milk successfully.

Why does my cat rub her face against things?

When a cat rubs against another cat or a human, it is her way of saying a friendly "hello". While she rubs, the cat spreads her scent over the other cat or human, and picks up some of their scent. When a cat rubs against furniture, she is using her scent to mark her territory.

Why does my cat play in the middle of the night?

Wild cats hunt early in the morning and during the night. This is when they can put their amazing night vision to good use (see pages 46–47). The hunting behaviour of wild cats has probably been passed down to our tame pet cats.

Why does my cat knead me with her paws?

Young kittens knead around their mother's teats to help the milk to come out. When they are older, cats use this kneading as a sign of affection. Cats also purr and sometimes drool as they knead. Every cat kneads differently – some use their claws and others don't. If your cat is clawing you while she kneads, put a cushion on your lap before letting her sit on you.

Why does my cat sleep so much?

Cats need exercise to stay healthy and use up a lot of energy when they do so. As a result, they also need a lot of sleep. An adult cat needs around 16 hours of sleep a day. This is why cats always seem to be napping. Cats become irritable if they do not get enough sleep.

🐾 Problem behaviour

Our pet cats can sometimes misbehave and act in ways that we don't like. The best way to stop unwanted behaviour is to try and understand why your cat is doing it. Then you can find a way of putting things right for her, and making life easier for both of you.

Attention seeking

Cats that feel they are not getting enough attention often miaow and howl, destroy things and scratch people. To stop this behaviour, have a set time of day that you spend only with your cat. Give her your full attention during this time, and do the things she enjoys best. At all other times, make sure you ignore your cat's bad behaviour and reward her good behaviour.

Ask the expert!

Q

Can I stop my cat bringing home dead animals?

A

No. Cats are natural hunters and may want to bring dead or alive animals home as trophies. Ask your vet for advice if you feel this is happening too often.

Aggression

Cats can sometimes become aggressive during play, by pouncing, batting, biting and scratching. This behaviour can cause injuries and should be discouraged. Often signs that your cat is about to become aggressive include tail swishing and flattened ears. When this happens, stop play immediately and walk out of the room. Cats can also become suddenly aggressive when they are on a person's lap being stroked. This often comes as a surprise, but there will be signs it is about to happen. These include tail twitching, flattened ears and a low growling.

When you notice one of these signs, stop stroking your cat immediately. Often, your stroking has made her feel trapped and she is ready to get down.

Spraying and soiling

Cats who spray or soil inside are usually feeling anxious about something and want to mark their territory. Soiling can occur when you move homes, and it is best to leave your cat in one room with a litter tray for the first few days. Cats often spray when a new pet, person, or piece of furniture is added to the home. Try to remove any object your cat repeatedly sprays on, or restrict her access to it. If your cat sprays in front of you do not respond, but instead clean it up when she has left the room. This lets her know that she cannot get your attention through spraying. Always take your cat to the vet if it is a new behaviour, or if you cannot think of any changes to the house that have caused it to happen.

Chapter 8: Grooming

🐾 Shorthaired cats

Cats are natural groomers who spend a large amount of time cleaning themselves. It's important you help with this task too. Groom your cat from when you first get her to keep her coat healthy and build a bond between you. Make sure there is always an adult present when you do any of these grooming activities.

Starting regular grooming from a young age will ensure your cat sees it as part of her routine and enjoys it.

Shorthaired cats

Shorthaired cats easily keep their coat free of dirt, debris and stray hairs by licking themselves. However, by grooming your cat once a week, you will help rid her coat of fleas and dead flakes of skin, and improve her circulation. It is important to groom your cat more frequently when she is moulting. This will remove any extra stray hairs that your cat may swallow otherwise. If swallowed, these hairs can build up and cause a fur ball, which may make your cat ill. Keep your grooming sessions to between five and ten minutes to begin with. You can extend this time as your cat gets used to being groomed. Never make it a negative experience, and ensure she has the option to escape if she needs to. Give her treats afterwards. If you do spot fleas while you are grooming, seek advice from your vet.

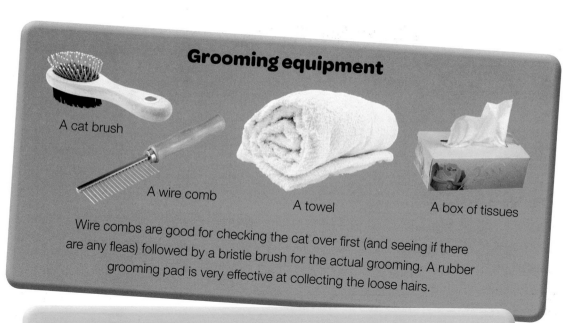

Grooming equipment

A cat brush

A wire comb

A towel

A box of tissues

Wire combs are good for checking the cat over first (and seeing if there are any fleas) followed by a bristle brush for the actual grooming. A rubber grooming pad is very effective at collecting the loose hairs.

Grooming your shorthaired cat

Groom your cat by placing a towel on your lap and inviting her to sit on you. Stroke your cat until she is relaxed before starting. Have a rubbish bin within arm's reach to put the stray hairs into.

1 Use a metal comb to comb your cat all over, which will remove any dead hairs, fleas and dirt. Make sure you wipe the comb clean afterwards with a tissue, which then goes into the bin.

2 Use a cat brush to brush gently along your cat's back and sides in the direction the fur grows.

3 Use the same brush to very carefully brush around your cat's sensitive areas: her stomach, armpits and around her tail and head.

Top tip!

If your cat stops grooming herself it is a sign something is wrong. If this happens, make sure she is taken to the vet.

🐾 Longhaired cats

Unlike shorthaired cats, longhaired cats cannot groom themselves properly. This means they need people to keep their coats clean and free from dirt, debris and tangles. Longhaired cats need to be groomed every day to stop their fur from becoming matted and uncomfortable.

Daily routine

It's best to make grooming your longhaired cat a set part of her daily routine. After a meal is often best, so your cat is feeling relaxed and lazy. Start the grooming sessions from the first day you get your cat. This will ensure that she gets used to being groomed and handled by you. Make the sessions only a few minutes long to start with, and extend them as time goes on.

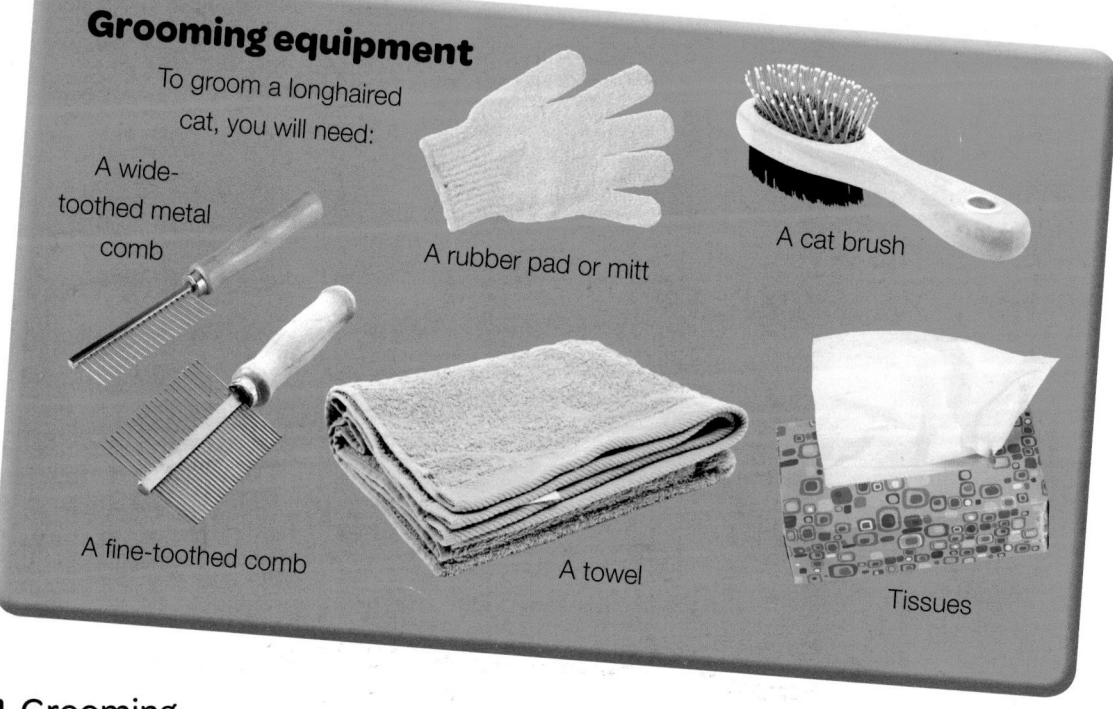

Grooming equipment

To groom a longhaired cat, you will need:

A wide-toothed metal comb

A rubber pad or mitt

A cat brush

A fine-toothed comb

A towel

Tissues

Grooming your longhaired cat

Groom your cat by placing a towel on your lap and inviting her to sit on you. Stroke your cat until she is relaxed before beginning. Have a rubbish bin within arm's reach to put the stray hairs into.

1 Use the wide-toothed comb along your cat's back and sides in the direction the fur grows. Don't cut out any knots (as you risk cutting the cat), but just tease them out slowly from the root with your fingers.

2 Use the wide-toothed comb to very carefully comb around your cat's sensitive areas: her stomach, armpits and around the head and tail.

3 Use the cat brush to brush your cat's back and sides in the opposite direction to how her fur grows.

4 Use a fine-tooth comb for the fur around your cat's neck, armpits, stomach, head and tail, combing in the opposite direction to how her fur grows. Wipe any debris or fleas off with a tissue.

5 Use a rubber pad or mitt to do a final brush to remove loose hairs.

Look out for signs that your cat is unhappy with grooming: tail swishing, body going tense, hissing or growling, licking lips or skin rippling.

Top tip!

While you are grooming your cat, wipe away any discharges from her eyes and ears with a tissue. Make sure you never put anything directly into your cat's eyes or ears.

Chapter 9: Biology and health

🐾 Cat anatomy

Cats have amazing bodies which are perfectly designed to survive life in the wild. Learning about your cat's body will help you better understand her. You'll also be more likely to notice if one of her body parts is not working properly.

Eyes

Cat eyes are specially adapted to see when there is very little light. They can see over eight times more than humans in dim light. This is why a cat's eyes seem to glow in the dark. It is the cat's eyes reflecting all of the available light.

Nose

Cats have an incredible sense of smell, which is over 40 times more powerful than a human's. As such, a cat can easily smell food, its prey and other cats.

Mouth

Cats are hunters and have a set of 30 teeth to kill prey and tear meat. A cat's tongue is covered with small, sharp spines which help her pull meat off bones and groom herself.

Whiskers

Cat whiskers are used to touch and feel things. With her whiskers, a cat can judge whether she can fit through a tight space. Her whiskers also pick up tiny changes in the air. This helps her move around objects in the dark, where the air is still.

Claws

Cats use their paws to attack, defend and climb. As such, a cat keeps her claws in top shape by sharpening them against trees and scratching posts. When they are not needed, a cat retracts her claws inside her paws. This allows her to move quietly, protects her claws and stops them becoming blunt.

Tail

A cat's muscular tail has several uses. It gives a cat her balance to climb, jump and walk across narrow spaces. It is also used as part of a cat's body language, which shows when she is happy, relaxed or angry.

Ears

A cat's hearing is many times better than a human's. A cat can swivel her ears in any direction and is able to pinpoint how far away a particular noise is. A cat's ears also help her balance, which allows her to land on all four feet.

🐾 Visiting the vet

As soon as possible after getting your cat you should take her to a vet. The vet will make sure your cat is healthy and book her in for vaccination injections. These protect your cat against diseases that she can catch from other cats.

Vaccinations

Kittens need to be vaccinated at nine weeks of age and again at 12 weeks of age. These vaccinations protect against diseases, such as feline leukemia (FeLV). After your cat has finished two rounds of vaccinations, she will need a booster injection every year. Your vet may also microchip your cat (see page 62) and treat her for worms (see pages 52–53) and fleas. Further worming should be carried out every three to six months to keep your cat healthy.

Top tip!

Take your cat to the vet at least once a year for her booster vaccinations and a check up.

Going to the vet

A visit to the vet can be stressful for your cat. For her, this means being locked in a cat carrier, a car journey, and then a waiting room full of animals. She then has to be handled and maybe injected by a stranger! Make the experience easier for you and your cat by following these tips.

Make her cat carrier a great place to go

Leave her carrier out at all times with the door open. Put a warm blanket inside and reward her with a treat when she goes inside. Leave a treat for her to find sometimes too. This way, getting into her carrier will not be an unpleasant experience.

Any friendly chatter will help calm your cat down and take the focus off her.

Make the waiting room calm

Keep the carrier on a seat (off the floor and away from any other animals) and ensure the basket is secured and covered with a blanket, so the cat feels it is safe in a hidey hole. If the waiting room is particularly noisy (dogs barking) ask if there is somewhere quieter for you to wait. Most veterinary practices will try to keep dogs and cats separate.

🐾 Cat neutering

When you first take your cat to the vet, you can discuss having her neutered. Neutering is an operation which stops your cat producing babies. It also helps protect your cat against disease and can prevent unwanted behaviour.

The operation

The neutering operation is performed by a vet on cats around four months of age. The operation is called 'spaying' for females and 'castration' for males. Unneutered males often stay away from home 'roaming', or looking for a mate. Unneutered males can also take on a strong 'tomcat smell'.

Unneutered females 'in season' miaow loudly to call a mate and have to be kept inside. Neutering can also stop cats from spraying to mark their territory and getting into fights. Often diseases are passed on through mating and fighting, so neutering reduces this risk. Without the need to have babies, neutered cats are often more affectionate and keen to spend time at home.

Why neuter

The main reason for neutering cats is to stop them having kittens. There are millions of unwanted kittens in the world and adding more of them stops the chance of them all finding homes. Female cats can start producing kittens from as young as four months old and can have three litters a year. There are usually three to five kittens in a standard litter. This means if a female cat gives birth to more females who then also breed, she could be responsible for thousands of cats!

Every year thousands of unwanted cats end up at rescue centres, such as Battersea Dogs & Cats Home. By neutering your cat, you will ensure you are not adding to this number.

Ask the expert!

Q

Is it kind to let my cat have one litter before neutering her?

A

No. In fact, neutering removes the stress of having kittens for female cats.

Top tip!

Never let your female cat outside if she is unneutered. She will almost certainly come back pregnant!

🐾 Common ailments

Cats are usually active, alert and healthy animals, who can heal themselves when sick. At other times, your cat may catch something that requires human help. When this happens, your cat will display some tell-tale symptoms that mean it's time to visit the vet.

Healthy or sick?

Check these cat body parts regularly for symptoms of illness. Also watch your cat's behaviour. If she is off her food, sleeping all the time, or moving awkwardly, it is best to take her to the vet.

Eyes
Eyes should be clear and open, not bloodshot, watery, or suffering from discharges.

Parasites

Parasites live on, or inside, your cat and should be removed. Normally, parasites can be prevented through regular treatment. At other times, symptoms will show further treatment is required.

Lice
Lice are biting insects like fleas, but white instead of reddish black.

Fleas
Fleas are tiny, biting insects that live in your cat's coat and which can make her itch like crazy. Ask your vet for the best treatment.

Ear mites
Mites live in your cat's ears and can cause itching, or a brown discharge. Visit the vet immediately if your cat displays these symptoms.

Worms

Worms are parasites that live inside your cat. Some come out like white noodles in your cat's poo. Cats should be regularly treated for worms, even if there are no symptoms. Ask your vet about the best worm treatments.

Top tip!

If your cat vomits up a dark, hairy ball don't panic. This is a fur ball and your cat is best rid of it!

Digestion system

Cats do vomit or get diarrhoea from time to time, but this should not persist for more than a day. If it does persist take her to your vet.

Teeth

Teeth should be white and clean, not yellow with inflamed gums.

Coat

Coats should be glossy and well groomed, not dirty, scruffy or bald in places.

Ears

Ears should be moving easily, standing upright and not itchy, patchy or suffering from discharges.

Chapter 10: On the move

🐾 Moving home

Cats are creatures of habit who like routine and familiar surroundings. Moving home can therefore be a huge upheaval for a cat. It's up to you to make the move as comfortable and relaxed as possible.

Packing up

Cats are curious animals and quick to notice change. Therefore, your cat will not consider people packing boxes and shifting furniture to be normal family behaviour. It is best to keep your cat inside for the few days before the move takes place. Leave her with her carrier, bed, toys, food and water bowls in one room, along with a litter tray. Make sure you give your cat lots of attention during this time.

Moving day

On the day of the move, take your cat's bed, toys, food and water bowls and litter tray and put them into one room in your new home. Drive over to your new home with your cat in her carrier. Introduce her to her room and keep her inside it for the first day. Put a few hidey holes in the room (cardboard boxes etc) as well as a few items of clothing that smell of the family so that she has familiar smells around her. Make sure you visit often to stroke her and give her treats.

Settling in

Let your cat into the rest of the house on the second day, but keep her inside for two weeks. This will give her time to explore her new home before seeing what's outside.

Ask the expert!

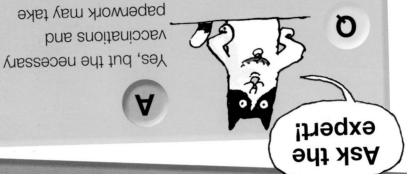

Q Can I take my cat abroad?

A Yes, but the necessary vaccinations and paperwork may take weeks to organise (see page 62 for pet passports).

Car travel

Cats do not like travelling by car, but if it happens regularly they will get used to it. Try these tips to make car travel a normal part of your cat's life.

- 🐾 Keep her carrier as far away from the engine as possible.
- 🐾 Put down a plastic sheet under her carrier in case she goes to the toilet.
- 🐾 Keep her carrier away from draughts, fans and heaters.
- 🐾 Keep your cat's favourite toys and cuddly blanket inside her carrier. Keep the carrier covered with a blanket.

- 🐾 Don't play loud music or make too much noise in the car as this may scare your cat.
- 🐾 If your cat gets sick on car journeys, don't feed her within an hour before you leave.
- 🐾 Keep your cat secure in her carrier at all times, never let her out, even if she seems very confident and unfazed by the experience.

Holidays

When you go on holiday you will need someone to look after your cat. Often a friend or family member can feed and check in on your cat while you are away. If this is not possible then your cat can stay in a cattery.

Staying at home

Having someone feed you cat while you are away is the best solution. This means your cat can stay in her own home and won't try and escape. However, having someone new look after her will be a change in her routine. For this reason, it is helpful to try a practice run before you go away.

While you are in the house, the person feeding your cat should let themselves in and give your cat some food. They should then spend some time stroking your cat. This will get your cat used to the person's smell and show her that they are friendly. Leave a list of what your cat eats and what she likes and dislikes. Make sure they have a way of contacting you while you are away.

Staying at a cattery

A cattery is like a hotel for a cat. Good catteries provide each cat with her own cabin and place to play, a litter tray and a warm bed. Often, a ramp takes the cat up to a bed near the ceiling, which comes with its own heater. Your vet will be able to suggest the best catteries in your area. It pays to book a cattery weeks or even months before you go away, as they quickly get full during holiday periods.

It's best to visit a cattery in advance and ask to be shown around. Make sure you are happy with the place and people who will be looking after your cat before you leave her there. Your cat will need to have had all of her vaccinations before she can stay at a cattery.

Top tip!

Make sure your cat feeder knows her 'dinner bell' sound, such as tapping on a tin or shaking a box of dried food (see page 28–29).

Chapter 11: Getting older

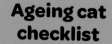 Old age

From the age of around 10 years old, your cat may begin to slow down. She may play less, sleep more, and her behaviour may change. This is because she has reached her old age.

Changing needs

From this point on, she will require extra care and attention as her needs change. It is a good idea to get your vet to check her over if you notice her slowing down. It may just be old age, but painful conditions such as arthritis can have the same effect and these can be treated by your vet. Once a cat is 12 years old, you should take her to the vet for regular health checks, as she can develop conditions that show no symptoms.

Ageing cat checklist

Provide one or more litter trays in the house.

Make sure you cat is always comfortable and warm.

Ask your vet to suggest a special diet.

Groom your cat gently to help her circulation.

Less active

As your cat gets older she may become less active and may put on weight. Being overweight as an older cat can lead to serious health problems. You can help prevent this by feeding your cat smaller meals more frequently. Buy a suitable food brand aimed at a 'senior' cat. She might also prefer softer foods. Your cat may not feel like jumping around, but playing simple games with her will help exercise her. Encouraging her to bat a toy on a string, for example, will keep your cat moving and entertained. Make sure you don't overtire your cat and let her rest whenever she wants to.

Saying goodbye

When cats get old, their bodies often stop working properly and they can suffer from painful ailments. In this case, sometimes the kindest thing is to let your vet end her life with an injection. This is a difficult decision, but better than seeing your beloved pet suffer and finding life too hard to bear. Saying goodbye is like losing a member of the family. It helps to look at photos and talk about all the good times you had together. Your family can decide how best to bury your cat and discuss this with your vet (see page 62 for burial information).

Top tip!

As your cat gets older she may become easily angry, miaow for no reason, or stare into space. Make sure you are always understanding of your cat's old age behaviour.

Ask the expert!

Q

How long do cats live?

A

Cats usually live for about 12–15 years, but some live to over 20.

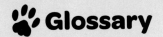 Glossary

Allergy
A physical reaction to something that doesn't agree with the body, such as cat hair.

Commitment
An ongoing obligation to carry something out.

Companion
A person or animal one spends a lot of time with.

Diarrhoea
Explosive, runny poo.

Discharge
Liquid waste material that often comes from the eyes, ears or nose.

Dispenser
A device that dispenses something, such as treats.

Housetrained
Trained to go to the toilet in a litter tray or outside of the house.

Kitten pen
A gated enclosure, such as a cage, to keep a cat in.

Litter tray
A plastic tray filled with special gravel or dirt where a cat goes to the toilet.

Microchipped
Inserting a microchip containing a special reference number into the scruff of a cat's neck. The microchip can be scanned to access the owner's details from a database.

Moulting
Shedding hair to make way for new growth.

Neutering
An operation that stops an animal from having babies.

Parasite
A tiny creature that lives in or on a bigger creature.

Rescue centre
A place that takes unwanted or homeless pets and rehomes them.

Roam
Move about over a wide area.

Social
Likes being around people or animals.

Socialisation
The process of introducing a cat to people and animals, so she becomes used to them.

Soiling
An animal having a poo inside.

Stray
An animal that does not have a home or an owner.

Temperament
An animal's nature which makes it behave the way it does.

Vaccination
A treatment to protect against disease.

Wean
To gradually stop giving milk to a baby animal and give it solid food instead.

Worms
A type of parasite that lives in a creature's stomach.

🐾 Helpful information

Microchipping

Microchipping involves injecting a microchip into the scruff of your cat's neck. The microchip has a unique number which is held in a central database with your contact details. Remember to update details when you move. This means when the microchip is scanned you can be contacted. Your vet or local council can microchip your cat. See the Battersea Dogs & Cats Home website for more information on microchipping: **battersea.org.uk.**

Collar and tag

Cats should wear a collar with an identification tag at all times. This means you can be contacted straight away if somebody finds your lost cat. Attaching a quick-release collar allows your cat to wriggle free if she becomes caught on something.

Duty of care

According to English law, you must:

🐾 Provide a suitable diet and environment for your cat.

🐾 Let your cat display normal behaviour.

🐾 Protect your cat from pain, suffering, injury and disease.

Cat travel abroad

Under the Pet Travel Scheme (PETS) your cat can travel within the EU and some other countries, if she has: been microchipped; had tapeworm treatment and a rabies vaccination; has a pet passport or official third country veterinary certificate. Your vet can issue your cat with a pet passport. For other countries there are different requirements, which can include blood tests and quarantine. More information can be found on the GOV.UK website:

https://www.gov.uk/take-pet-abroad

Top tip!

Pet insurance is highly recommended to make sure the cost of your cat's vet bills are covered. See the Battersea Dogs & Cats Home website for more information.

🐾 About Battersea

Battersea Dogs & Cats Home looks after 6,000 dogs and 3,000 cats every year and is one of the oldest and most famous rescue centres in the world. We have been caring for lost, unwanted and neglected animals since 1860. We have three centres, in Battersea, at Old Windsor in Berkshire and in Brands Hatch, Kent. We aim never to turn away an animal in need, and our carers, vets, nurses and 1,000 volunteers make sure all our residents are loved and cared for while we try to find them loving new homes. Visit our website at **battersea.org.uk** to find out more about us.

Index